DISCARDED

W9-DBF-652

SULZER REGIONAL

THE WRITINGS OF

WILL ROGERS

I - 4

SPONSORED BY

The Will Rogers Memorial Commission
and Oklahoma State University

THE WRITINGS OF WILL ROGERS

OTHER VOLUMES TO BE ANNOUNCED

WILL ROGERS MEMORIAL COMMISSION

Raymond W. Knight, *Chairman* Irving Fisher
Robert W. Love Harry Hoagland
Roy G. Cartwright Will Rogers, Jr.
David R. Milsten
Governor David Boren, *ex-officio*

MEMORIAL STAFF

Reba Neighbors Collins, Delmar Collins,
Curator Manager

SPECIAL CREDIT

The late Paula McSpadden Love
Curator, 1938-73

OSU ADVISORY COMMITTEE

Odie B. Faulk, *Chairman* John W. Hamilton
E. Moses Frye Howard R. Jarrell
Marvin T. Edmison Roscoe Rouse
George A. Gries
President Robert B. Kamm, *ex-officio*

EDITORIAL CONSULTANTS

Ray B. Browne, *Bowling Green State University*
LeRoy H. Fischer, *Oklahoma State University*
Wilbur R. Jacobs, *University of California,
Santa Barbara*
Howard R. Lamar, *Yale University*
Russel B. Nye, *Michigan State University*

ROGERS-ISMS

The Cowboy Philosopher
on THE PEACE
CONFERENCE

By Will Rogers

Joseph A. Stout, Jr., *Editor*
Peter C. Rollins, *Assistant Editor*

OKLAHOMA STATE UNIVERSITY PRESS
Stillwater, Oklahoma
1975

© 1975 Oklahoma State University Press

Note to scholars: The Harper & Brothers book and the original illustrations are reproduced with permission of the Will Rogers Memorial Commission, Claremore, Oklahoma, and The Rogers Company, Beverly Hills, California. The scholarly apparatus and notes in this volume are copyrighted and the usual rules about the use of copyrighted material apply.

*(Illustrations courtesy Will Rogers Memorial,
Claremore, Oklahoma)*

D
646
.R6
Cop.1

International Standard Book Number 0-914956-05-1

Library of Congress Catalog Number 75-8471

Printed in the United States of America

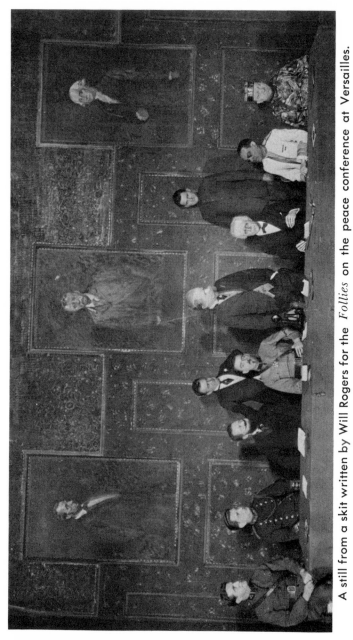

A still from a skit written by Will Rogers for the *Follies* on the peace conference at Versailles.

CONTENTS

INTRODUCTION

Historical Context: America and the Great War

Woodrow Wilson became President of the United States on March 4, 1913, amid an era of prosperity and American exuberance for the future. Before his administration ended eight years later, the country had watched while the Mexican and Russian revolutions drastically altered those countries, and a great world war had threatened the existence of all peace loving people. Throughout these experiences Americans, too, were changing. After the Spanish-American War the United States had begun to share the responsibilities of world leadership, ultimately becoming involved in World War I.

For several years, Europe had been drenched in volatile national rivalries. Then in the summer of 1914 a conflagration was started by a spark from the Balkans—a long standing trouble spot. The Austria-Hungary block declared war on Serbia in July, 1914, for allegedly harboring terrorists who assassinated Austrian Archduke Franz Ferdinand. Germany supported Austria. Russia then joined the war because it had pledged to protect Serbia. Germany next declared war on Russia and its ally, France. Immediately after German armies crashed through neutral Belgium to attack France, Great Britain was drawn into the confict. By the end of 1914, the entire continent was at war.

An imbalance of power, a clash of economic interests, a rising tide of nationalism, and the ugly head of militarism all had contributed to the fire of war. When war began, Americans were horrified and looked upon the imbrogilo as just another remote European quarrel. The United States struggled desperately for more than two years to remain aloof. But the aggressions of Germany and the fires of war eventually made American intervention necessary.

On April 1, 1917, President Wilson reluctantly asked Congress to "declare the recent course of the Imperial German Government to be in fact nothing less than war against the Government and the people of the United States." The First World War lasted only a few months after the United States became a participant, but during these months more than two million Americans served in Europe. World War I ended on November 11, 1918. As soon as the shooting was over, a new struggle began —a diplomatic struggle to build a lasting peace.

Wilson had tried to keep the United States out of the war, but once the decision to become involved was made, he devoted the nation to the struggle as "a war to end all wars." Several months before the armistice and before the United States had mobilized sufficiently to force a peace settlement, Wilson announced his vision for a stable world order. On January 8, 1918, the President addressed a joint session of Congress, outlining his famous fourteen points.

The Germans were unwilling to heed the President's offer because they had just defeated the Russians on the Eastern Front. The Central Powers hoped that this victory in the East would allow them to mass forces in the West before American troops could reach the continent. When this final bloody German assault on France was turned back, all parties became aware that German defeat was inevitable. On October 18, 1918, the Central Powers suddenly acknowledged an interest in Wilson's peace plan.

In the middle of these peace maneuverings, the Congressional election of 1918 was held in the United States. Wilson publicly appealed to the American people to elect a Democratic Congress so that he could negotiate with power. Ignoring this

Presidential appeal, the voters returned Republican majorities both to the House and Senate. On November 18, 1918, the President announced that he would attend the Paris Peace Conference as head of the American delegation. With consummately poor judgment of political realities, Wilson chose his peace commissioners almost entirely from Democratic ranks. Colonel Edward House, Secretary of State Robert Lansing, General Tasker H. Bliss, and Henry White, the only Republican, were the commissioners. All of them were able men, but diplomatic and political circumstances demanded more than ability. What was needed was a peace commission that was bi-partisan, and therefore representative of Congress and the voters' wishes.

With his chosen commissioners, Wilson boarded the *George Washington* early in December. On December 13, 1918, he reached Brest; from there to Paris he was given a hero's welcome. Before the peace conference met, Wilson briefly visited England and Italy receiving wide acclaim wherever he journeyed. Getting the peace negotiations underway was yet another matter, for the conference was delayed until January 13, 1919. When the sessions began, it was clear that at least two irreconcilable positions plagued any treaty settlement. Wilson's idealism was contained in his famous Fourteen Points where he emphasized a recognition of the rule of law and a sensitivity to the aspirations of European nationalism. The representatives of France, England, and Italy ignored these ideals and focused instead on punishing Germany. While Wilson had called for open agreements among nations, he was completely unaware that several of the European Allies already had signed secret treaties containing territorial promises of strategic and economic importance. Despite these serious obstacles, Wilson was willing to sacrifice almost every other point of his peace plan in order to promote a League of Nations. Wilson hoped that the League would establish a rule of law among nations and thereby avert future world conflicts over land and national hatreds.

Unfortunately, Wilson's goals were not only thwarted at the conference, but also his plan for American involvement in the League of Nations was destroyed. Opposition to the treaty and the League in the Senate was sufficient to block ratification of the President's treaty. Wilson tried every means in his power to promote the League, including a country-wide speaking tour. The pressure of war, negotiations, and a partisan, recalcitrant Congress took its toll on the President, for he collapsed on September 26, 1919, after speaking in Pueblo, Colorado. Possibility of United States participation in the League of Nations ended during November when the treaty was officially defeated in the Senate. The peace treaty between the Central Powers and the Allies was signed at Paris on January 20, 1920; there was no representative from the United States present. The Americans technically were still at war with the enemy. Ultimately, newly inaugurated President Warren G. Harding was forced to support legislation declaring the world contest officially over. Congress declared the war ended on July 2, 1921.

The Cowboy Philosopher on the Peace Conference exhibited Will Rogers' earliest manner of comic delivery. Nevertheless, the book demonstrated that Rogers could say things clearly and humorously. It might well be also that Rogers did not write this book in the traditional sense; rather the work could have been assembled from notes Rogers sent to the publisher.

The Rogers Posture: A Friend of Men in Power

In 1915, Will Rogers was assigned to the Midnight Frolic portion of Ziegfeld's Follies. Because the audience included wealthy New Yorkers and visiting dignitaries, it provided a special challenge to a humorist, for many of those who attended could afford to return night after night. As a result, Rogers was forced to change his material every evening. One way of changing—suggested by his wife Betty—was to build gags around contemporary events. As the humorist stated in the introductory note to this book, he was always received well by men of real power: "you can always joke about a big Man that is really big." After Rogers became more adept at the satirical style, he applied his verbal lasso to bigger game. Instead of simply jesting at patrons who appeared at the Follies, he applied the same sort of familiar criticism to figures of national importance. This book demonstrated continuous evidence of the new, bolder style. For example, Rogers asserted that the President talked to him about traveling to Versailles with the Peace Commission: "I still wanted to go along, but he said: 'Wait till some other trip and I will take you'." Financier Bernard Baruch was just plain "Barney." Rogers stated that Josephus Daniels was allowed to travel to Europe, but that he would only behave himself "in a Crowd." And Secretary of War Newton Baker was described as returning to France because "Old Newt kinder likes Paris."

For Rogers' audience, there was a twofold appeal of this verbal assertion of familiarity. It indicated that Rogers knew these powerful figures and that he could discern their motives. Morever, the fact that he spoke of them by nickname rather than their official titles reduced the sense of distance between Rogers' audience and these great men.

Layers of Rogers' Humor

The humor of *The Cowboy Philosopher at the Peace Conference* was related to more than the failings of Woodrow Wilson's gallant peace efforts.

On the most superficial level, Rogers' humor played upon the simple human comedy of such a polyglot gathering. These observations were concocted to delight rather than instruct. There was the familiar Rogers device of developing a parallel between politicians and show business celebrities. Speaking of Wilson's triumphal tour of Italy, Rogers explained that the President was well greeted not because he symbolized Europe's intense nationalistic aspirations, but simply because "He had a letter of recommendation from Caruso." Then there were the human problems entailed in the confrontation of vastly different cultures: "Let's hope the Turkish Delegation don't bring all their WIVES or we never will get PEACE." Finally, Rogers underscored how difficult it was for the average American to keep track of all of these complex European developments: "Now the Pres says we are going to recognize the CZECHO SLOVAKS. We may recognize them but we will never pronounce them."

But there was a dark side of Will Rogers' observations, one which emphasized that human viciousness rather than Wilsonian idealism was triumphing at the diplomatic tables. Rogers was especially caustic about the Japanese: "The Japanese have offered to protect Siberia if they have to stay there forever." Rogers was disappointed that the recognition of nationalism was not leading to greater harmony, but more conflict: "The Czechoslovaks have gotten their freedom, I see where they are at war." In what may have been the climax of this expression, Rogers summarized his sense of the tragic absurdity of the entire meeting: "And they call THAT A PEACE CONFERENCE." Here he emphasized the unwillingness of mankind's official leaders to live up to their promises.

President Wilson's inability to implement many of his highly publicized Fourteen Points elicited some of Will Rogers' most acerbic remarks: "See where Pres. Wilson and Italy compromised on that town down there *Italy got it.*" Using the same comic device, Rogers communicated his further irritation with the success of Japan at the conference: "See where Pres. Wilson and Japan compromised on the CHOW CHOW PLACE JAPAN GETS IT." Rogers believed that what really lay behind the facade of the "peace conference" was a rapacity which could be satisfied by neither well-meaning declarations nor presidential charisma. From Rogers' common sense point of view, Wilson's verbal fog invited more Machiavellian members of the Big Four to devour Europe. In these dark moments, Rogers revealed that he placed little faith in American idealism: "They agreed on one of the Fourteen Points that was that America went in for nothing and expects nothing. They are all unanimous WE GET IT." Rogers recognized that Wilson was surrendering on so many points because he hoped that a League of Nations somehow would transform the international jungle into a law-abiding community of nations, but the Oklahoman questioned constructing a world of peace on the foundations of reprisals and reparations.

The Rogers Gift: Reducing Anxiety

Rogers in this book demonstrated a special ability to translate complex, impersonal problems into comprehensible metaphors. This translation clarified problems, and thereby postured the mind of his audience toward constructive thought. In a lighter vein, Rogers noted that even the announcement of an armistice could have comic, human results: "Of course, we got the word a couple of days before it was really signed, Making everybody have TWO DRUNKS where one would have done just as well." Or Rogers could play upon the human irony of the fate of monarchy in the Twentieth Century: "Kaiser and Czar used to kid King George and tell him he dident have any power. He can get back at them now and say 'No I havent got much power, but I am *kinging* it, ain't I?' "

At more serious moments, Rogers attempted to penetrate the official rhetoric of world leaders to the timeless human motives at work. Late in this book, he swept all of the 800,000 words of the Versailles Treaty and all of Wilson's Fourteen Points aside in favor of a metaphor straight out of rural American experience. He stated simply that the Allies "could have settled the whole thing in one sentence, 'If you BIRDS START ANYTHING AGAIN WE WILL GIVE YOU THE OTHER BARREL.' " Speaking in equally familiar terms to the readers, Rogers translated the fundamental tragedy of Versailles. President Wilson may have hoped for a new Europe, but the treaty was a disaster for anyone capable of making a realistic assessment of the political future of the continent. In Rogers' unequivicable terms, "I thought the Armistice terms read like a second Mortgage, But this reads like a FORCLOSURE." While students of international politics could reasonably complain that Rogers oversimplified the complex issues, it is clear that the translations provided by his journalism helped Americans to confront their problems in human terms. Humor, of course, was his primary goal. But Rogers' journalism made pressing current issues clearly identifiable and manageable for his audience.

Finally, *The Cowboy Philosopher at the Peace Conference* not only marked a special moment in Will Rogers' career—his movement from stage comic to author—but the book revealed some of the basic ingredients of his humor: Rogers' humor helped close the gap between Americans and their leaders; Rogers' humor could entertain, but it served equally well to indict human selfishness; Rogers' employment of metaphors from everyday life brought abstract problems to the level of average comprehension. For these reasons, the audience for Will Rogers' journalism grew as his output increased.

We are extremely grateful to the Kerr-McGee Foundation, Phillips Petroleum Corporation, Mr. and Mrs. Robert W. Love. Mrs. T.S. Loffland, and the Legislature of the State of Oklahoma for their continued support of this project.

THE EDITORS

The unveiling of the Will Rogers bust at Oklahoma City's Will Rogers Airport, 1952. (*L to R*) Sylvan N. Goldman, Charles Nesbitt, Stanley Draper and Henry L. Bellmon.

PREFACE

It was not my privilege ever to shake hands with Will Rogers, yet today, I feel that I knew him well. Perhaps it is best that I had no personal association with the Cherokee genius, for my heartfelt admiration of him is far deeper than any casual brush with him could have engendered.

Will Rogers was a one-time man. Like few men in all of history he can never be duplicated. In all of his activities he was himself—as a cowboy, a stage star, a motion picture pioneer, a writer, a radio entertainer or a banquet speaker or lecturer, he was always just Will Rogers. And Will Rogers was always great.

I remember when I returned from France at the end of World War I, I saw Will Rogers in the Ziegfeld Follies in New York. Standing in the spotlight on the huge stage twirling his lariat the Oologah, Oklahoma cowboy eased the memories of St. Mihiel and the Meuse-Argonne Forest in the mind of a still young Oklahoma soldier. Then, as through all of his spectacular career, he kept his often hilarious quips as up to date as the latest newspaper. No person held a position too high for him to needle or praise in a way no one since can match.

During the decade of the tumultuous Twenties my brother, Alfred, and I were in business in Tulsa. Early in 1930 we moved from Tulsa to Oklahoma City to make a new start. Times were tough; the depression years were difficult and discouraging. Nature's dust bowl compounded all of the problems.

Will Rogers' daily telegram published in *The Daily Oklahoman* made life a little brighter, his radio programs poked fun at our leaders and he injected his wholesome home-spun philosophy that made the country feel a bit better. America pulled itself together and by the mid-thirties the sun was beginning to peek through.

Then Will Rogers died, along with another great Oklahoman, Wiley Post, in an airplane crash near Point Barrow, Alaska, on August 15, 1935. The nation was stunned. The Oklahoma home-folks were desolate.

Yet Will Rogers' works live on.

Promptly the Oklahoma Legislature passed a bill to put up a statue of Will Rogers in Statuary Hall in the nation's capitol in Washington, D. C., so he can forever keep his eyes on the senators and congressmen, and they will know he is watching their every antic. The internationally famous sculptor, Jo Davidson, was selected to do it.

And Will Rogers was to come home. A committee of prominent citizens led a successful effort to establish and finance the Will Rogers Memorial at Claremore and the boy from Oologah who roped the world now rests in a sarcophagus, in a garden, by the handsome memorial which stands where he would have built his home, if he ever could have settled down.

The Will Rogers Memorial is eloquently described as the finest thing ever done by Oklahomans for an Oklahoman.

I remember the day when a tremendous gathering —more than 20,000 people, Indians, cowboys and other friends of Will Rogers—came from all over for the unveiling of the second casting of Jo Davidson's magnificent statue in the rotunda of the Memorial designed and built by John Duncan Forsyth.

As a part of the unveiling ceremony President Franklin D. Roosevelt, speaking from Washington on the coast-to-coast radio broadcast, put into simple words the meaning of Will Rogers:

"There was something infectious about his humor. His appeal went straight to the hearts of the nation. Above all things, in a time grown too solemn and sober, he brought his countrymen back to a sense of proportion."

That day, those words, and the vivid memory as the light fell just right on the statue as it was unveiled, remained with me and later gave me the golden opportunity to honor Oklahoma's favorite son, who said, "I never met a man I didn't like."

In the early fall of 1950, at an Oklahoma City Chamber of Commerce Goals for Oklahoma City planning meeting, I heard E. K. Gaylord, publisher of *The Daily Oklahoman* and *Oklahoma City Times,* comment that there was not even a photograph of Will Rogers at our airport which is named for him. Memories flooded back and I got busy. A bronze bust from the mold of the original Will Rogers statue would be ideal for display in the airport. I would be proud to make such a gift to my hometown. My friend R. Morton Harrison, a longtime friend of Will Rogers and a prominent member of the Memorial Commission, was also a friend of Jo Davidson. I asked Harrison if he could tell me where to reach the sculptor. He located him in New York.

Davidson advised us he had not been in Paris since before World War II started and the molds of the statue were left in his studio there. He was going to Paris soon and would search for them. On December 23, 1950, Davidson wrote, "The Will Rogers mold is intact."

We were overjoyed and negotiated with him for a bust which he agreed to finish as soon as he completed his scheduled works. One year later in the last week of December, 1951, the bronze bust arrived in Oklahoma City. In less than a week, on January 2, 1952, Jo Davidson died in France. The bust displayed in Oklahoma City's Will Rogers World Airport, is one of the last pieces of the great sculptor's work.

Since then it has been my privilege to have three more casts made from that mold which were presented to the Tulsa Municipal Airport, at their request, the State of Oklahoma for display in the Will Rogers Capitol Office Building in Oklahoma City, and the National Cowboy Hall of Fame and Western Heritage Center in Oklahoma City.

Shortly after dedication ceremonies of the bust at the Tulsa Memorial Airport, I was contacted by Dr. R. W. Knight, then principal of the Will Rogers High School in Tulsa. Students there had, for some time, been trying to raise money to buy an original painting of Will Rogers—the only one he ever sat for. They were having a problem, so I agreed to purchase it for them. The beautiful portrait by Count Arnaldo Tamburini, Court Artist of Italy, was unveiled by Will Rogers, Jr. in impressive ceremonies at the school on January 27, 1954.

Through these bits of art it has been my joy to help preserve the memory of Oklahoma's greatest son so he will always be fresh in the minds of generations yet unborn. To those of my generation, however, Will Rogers is, perhaps, summed up ideally in these lines by Ogden Nash:

> I worked with gum and grin and lariat
> To entertain the proletariat,
> And with my Oklahomely wit
> I brightened up the earth a bit.

He did, indeed.

Sylvan N. Goldman

The Cowboy Philosopher
on *The Peace Conference*

I - 4

IN the Five times I have appeared before President Wilson I have used dozens of these
same jokes, about him, And he
has the best sense of humor and
is the best audience I ever
played too, Which bears out
the theory I work on, That you
can always joke about a big
Man that is really big, But
dont ever kid about the little
fellow that thinks he is something, cause he will get sore
Thats why hes little,

W.R.

ALIBI

THERE is no particular reason why I should horn in on you Public with a Book, But thats just when they seem to write them, When theres no need or reason for them,

The shorter white Paper gets the more careless these Pen Hounds get with it,[1]

All my friends advise me to go ahead Will and write it cause you wont annoy people with it like these other Writers do with theirs, Nobody will read yours

When a Guy has never grazed educationally any further than McGuffeys fourth Reader[2] his ravings aint liable to throw any jealous scare into Literary Circles,

Grammar and I get along like a Russian and a Bath Tub,

In fact Americans are getting to dote too much on Grammar and Good Manners, They say the most perfect English in this country is spoken in Sing Sing, And at the

1

Federal Prison in Atlanta, They claim a
Knife never touched a Lip, So you see where
that junk leads you too,

I was going to write a Book on the War,
But I heard some fellow had already done it,

In fact I figure that the fellow who dont
write on the war will be a novelty,

There is so many Books on the War that no two
people will have to read the same Book.

Then the War was too serious a subject
I could not write on it, But the Peace Feast,
That seemed to offer a better field for Humor
provided you stick to the *facts*,

I have some inside facts procured from the
most reliable source, And as I dont want to
see the World grow up in ignorance on this
historical subject I would really feel selfish
and mean too withold it,

Heres how I got it, There is a fellow I
know, Who had a friend, And this friends
Sister had a sweetheart and he was a Soldier

in France and his cousins pal was a Bunkie of Col Houses[3] Chouffer, The Col told his Chouffer So you see my information comes from the same place Pres Wilsons[4] does,

So Here Goes Under The Bottom With THE FIRST PEACE BOOK,

THE
PEACE CONFERENCE

OF course this whole Peace Conference talk started from the time Pres Wilson said to Germany "We wont deal with you as long as you occupy invaded Territory." Well the Kaiser[5] come right back at him and said, "If you can show us how we can give it up any faster than we are I wish you would do it,"

Now the Armistace was signed, and Germany agreed to quit running at eleven oclock on a certain day,

Of course we got the word a couple of days before it was really signed, Making everybody have **TWO DRUNKS** where one would have done just as well,[6]

It would have been signed on this first day But the German Generals whom they sent out to sign up, had never been to the front and dident know just where it was,

The Kaiser was on the verge at one time of visiting the western front then he said, "No I will just wait a few days till it comes to me,"

Our Show was playing in Philadelphia
when the first Armistace was signed, (*The
one the saloon man framed up*) I was a bit
leary of it all the time as I had been there
once before when the Union League Club[7]
had paraded for a Mr. Hughes,[8] Then later
they had to put the Parade back,

I HAD ALWAYS BELIEVED PHILA TO BE SLOW
AND HERE IT WAS 2 DAYS AHEAD OF THE FACTS

At that time everybody wondered what
to do with the Kaiser, I thought he should
have been brought to this Country and made
to clean the streets after that first Armistace
day,

A funny thing the Armistace was signed
about the time the returns of the last election
come in. The Germans and the Democrats
learned their fate on the same day,

When the war was over the Kaiser called
his 6 sons to him and said, "Now boys we
better duck Cause this war is over and you
boys can get hurt *Now*,"[9]

The thing that hurt the Kaiser worse than
losing the war, Was that in all the Armistace
terms they dident even mention his name,

Everybody commence talking about the Peace Conference and who was to go, Some Republican Senators went so far as to engage a lower birth,

There was so much argument about who was to go, That Pres Wilson says I tell you what, "We will split 50-50 I will go and you fellows can stay,"[10]

At last we were going to get even with them for all their commissions coming over here,

You know for a while COMMISSIONS were coming so fast, That we were lucky to find a fellow who knew what Flag to put out each day,

We were meeting Servian Commissions with Romanian Flags,

Of course there were nations coming at that time who had not enough to support a flag, Thats why the commission were here to place a Flag Contract,

Now to get to my Peace trip, About three months are supposed to have elapsed between

the last Paragraph and this one, All of which
time was taken up by Congress talking, *(see
congressional Record)* Finally Pres Wilson
got tired listening to them and walked out on
them,

If it had not been to get away from Congress, I have my doubts if he would have
gone to Europe,

Now for the Number 2 Peace trip,

This Peace trip is not an original Idea,
(It was originated by some obscure MANA-
FACTURER OF KNICK NACKS,) *Name furnished
at advertising rates,*[11]

Its always the same, the fellow who orig-
inates anything or starts something new is
generally called a nut, The next fellow comes
along takes his Idea improves on it and of
course is a smart man,

Of Course this No 2 Company used better
Judgement than the first one. This one
waited till the war was over to Go,

This is the only case in Theatrical History
where the No 2 Company was better than the
original,

The Peace Conference

Of corse I claim this Manafacturer in some middle west town (I cant seem to recall that fellows name) made one mistake, There were people on his Boat that should never have had a return trip ticket,

Through Holland receiving them is where the Kaiser got his idea of going there,

Of course there was a lot of dissatisfaction against the Pres going, Mostly by people whom he did not take along,

I was in favor of his going because I thought it would give us a chance to find out who was Vice President,[12] But it Dident,

I also felt confident that he was the only man that could explain the 14 points[13]

_ _

We were especially lucky in having him represent us in England as he is the only one we could have sent that spoke good enough english that they could understand,

He would have taken a Senator but couldent find one that had a dress Suit

A congressman of course was out of the question He couldent have eaten off a 15 million dollar plate He would have starved to death looking at it,

For awhile it looked like Mr Hughes would get to go, While the others were signing up he could have been investigating, his report would have been ready the day before the next election,

Also asked a manafacturer from some lake town (I cant think of that Birds name) But he said "No thank you one trip cured me"

The Sectry of Agriculture[14] was named to go for a while, It was thought that if we were fortunate enough to be assigned any loose Islands at the meeting He could immediately advise what to plant thereby getting in a crop next year,

MR ROOT[15] was named then some one happened to think of RUSSIA and that was off,

Wanted BRYAN to go but nobody knew where he was,[16]

10

The Peace Conference

I wanted to go along as *JESTER* Pres Wilson will miss his comedy when he gets away from Congress,

I wanted to represent the United Press (the one that sent in that prematur peace report) I could have had them there before they started,

See they took one Republican with them, But I have never read any thing in the papers about him landing, Just about chucked that guy overboard,

Took a republican along to argue with on the way over,

They will about make him Wait on the Peace Table,

See where Admiral Dr Grayson stood his Maiden voyage well,[17]

Mr Creel went along to suppress any SCANDAL that may crop up[18]

On arriving they found they had forgotten something after searching they found it was the *Industrial Committee,*

Now Mr Barney Baruch is going in case we
land a few Shekels, why Barney will count
up for us,[19]

*Also Mr Garfield "said he wasent going to
stay in this Country and FREEZE another
winter,"*[20]

If they keep on sending for them, Talk
about getting the boys back, it will take a
couple of years to get all these Peace Guys
back,

We may not have had as many Nations in
the war as these other Nations but we are
going to Swamp them at the Peace Table,

Col House was there to meet the Boat in a
listening Capacity,

Lot of men have *fought* their way into
fame and *talked* their way into fame but Col
House is the only man that ever just LISTENED
HIMSELF IN,

After looking over Paris the troop went to
London, Can you imagine how sore these
Republicans got when they read about a
Democrat sleeping in Buckingham Palace,

12

Kaiser and Czar used to kid King George and tell him he dident have any power He can get back at them now and say "No I havent got much power but I am still *Kinging* aint I,"[21]

Pres left London passed through Paris got an earfull from Col House and played a week of one Night stands through Italy,

He had a letter of recomendation from Caruso[22] so he met some of the best people in Italy,

Every time the Pres wanted applause in his speeches in Italy he would mention GARIBALDI which sounds same in English as Italian,[23]

Belgium wanted to book him there but the Pres got wise that they were holding so many Banquets they were trying to wear him out before the Peace Feast started,

King of Italy[24] also the King of England have agreed with him up to now But unfortunately they neither one will be at the Peace signing,

England is orally in accord but there has been nothing signed,

They are a little late starting as they were waiting to find someone who knew what freedom of the Seas mean,

NOW IF HE CAN ONLY HANDLE THAT MEET-ING AS HE DOES CONGRESS WE NEED HAVE NO FEAR OF THE RESULT,

You know a lot of people think he is liable to be too easy with them dont you believe it he can be pretty stern when he wants to remember last fall when he sent Germany their Questionaire, Said GIVE ME YOUR REAL NAME AND PERMANENT AD-DRESS,[25]

Lets hope the Turkish Deligation dont bring all their WIVES or we never will get *PEACE,*

And lets make those Russians shave before they sign up we want to know who we are dealing with,

If Ireland sends a deligation I can hear France say bring us back war,

Now the Pres says we are going to rec-ognize the CZECHO SLOVAKS we may recognize them but we will never pronounce them,

That Nation has caused Readers more trouble than any other one in war,

They cant make the Peace terms much worse than those Armistace terms for they read like a 2nd mortgage, Party of the second part has no more chance than a Democrat in the next Congress,

We are handicapped at this meeting, England and France both have their Prime Ministers there while *BILLY SUNDAY* dident go for us,[26]

Each Nation is supposed to share in the Peace terms according to what they have done in the war, Holland gets the KAISER, Mexico the CROWN PRINCE,[27]

Now the Pres has to get back here before Mar 1st when the Country goes in into the hands of the Republicans or they are liable to want to charge him a tarriff to get in again,

OF COURSE WE DONT RECEIVE MUCH NEWS OF THE PEACE CONFERENCE. FIRST FEW WEEKS THEY ARE ALL JUST COMPLIMENTING EACH OTHER. WAIT TILL THEY GO TO DIVIDE UP SOMETHING. (What a truth that turned out to be)

15

Well by this time Congress was getting pretty rough so Pres W grabbed his boat and commuted back home,[28]

Said I think I will land in BOSTON the old Pilgrim Fathers had pretty fair luck, and *nobody has ever landed there since,*

Germany couldent figure out how America could get troops over there and get them trained so quick they dident know that in our manual there is nothing about RETREATING and when you only got to teach an Army to go one way you can do it in half the time,

I feel pretty proud over that last little gag, As I used it before Pres Wilson in Washington and he repeated it in his Boston speech, Saying "as one of our AMERICAN HUMORISTS says," Up to then I had only been an ordinary Rope thrower,[29]

Pretty tough when the Pres cops your act,

Pres had pretty good luck on that 1st trip they saw his 14 points and raised him _____ more[30]

Says in there, "There is to be no more wars" and then there was a Paragraph a little further down told you where to get your AMMUNITION in case there was one,

Now he come's back to Washington to explain the *LEAGUE OF NATIONS* to Congress   You know those guys cant read anything and understand it,

But after eating out of 15 million dollar Gold Plates and hobnobbing with Kings and Dukes can you imagine how Congress looked to him when he come back,

Had All the Senators up to dinner at White House   Took Ham Lewis three days to dress for it,[31]

Not much news from the Dinner Burleson copped the Phones,[32]

On last day went up to Capitol to sign all the bills Congress had passed Well after he had signed the *bill.*

Then he went before Congress and balled out the WILFUL 37,[33] he was busier than Mcadoo with a new train,[34]

HE and Taft both spoke on same stage first time Pres and x-pres ever *agreed,*[35]

I still wanted to go along but he said: "wait Will till some other trip and I will take you,"

17

You know 13 is his lucky number if they dont sign this up on this trip he knows they will on his 13th trip,

You see Congress got sore cause he did not call them in extra session, You know the next Con, is *Republican,* Be a good joke on them if he dident call them at all wouldent it,

Back to Paris to meet Col House the only man the Pres ever listened too,

MR DANIELS went over.[36] First time they have ever taken Josephus anywhere, He will be allright in a crowd,

Made Mr Hoover food DICTATOR for all the Allies   That means that *BELG FRANCE* and *ENG,* are not going to get any *more* to eat than we do,[37]

Conference at 1st gave America Japan Italy France 5 deligates each and England including her Colonies fourteen, Thats all right to allow England for each one of her *Foreign Relations,* But they did not allow us a single one for *Wisconsin,*[38]

How would you like to have been on a committee of Englishman *to inform Ireland they dident get any Deligates,* OH BOY,[39]

Finally got it down to the big TEN now theres only FOUR, speaking to each other,[40]

America dident know till they got over there that those European Nations have had a disease for years called the **Gimmes.**

England and Japan had a secret Treaty where England was to get everything south of the equator and Japan everything North, Guess they were going to leave the equator for Ireland,[41]

Japan wanted to put in the contract that she was as good as anybody else If she *admitted* it why put it in, If a man is a Gentleman he don't have a *sign* on him telling it,

Tell Japan we will recognize them as soon as they recognize China,

Peace Table is turning out like all Banquets the speeches are too long,

Everybody at the Table wants a second helping, And Germany the cook hasent got enough to go around,

They agreed on one of the 14 points that was that America went in for *nothing* and *expects nothing* they are all UNANIMOUS WE GET IT,

Wanted to put the LEAGUE of nations in with Peace Treaty, thats like a fellow going into a store and the Merchant wont sell him a Suit unless he uses a Gillette Razor,

Its been a great thing for these Senators if it had not been for this to *knock* they would not have gotten all these Lecture Dates,

The way a lot Of Senators talk you would think Pres W was going to trade America off for a couple of Golf Clubs,

They seem to think the Pres took the **Monroe Doctrine** in his pocket and is liable to lose it over there,[42]

Pres Wilson threatened he would start the war over again, Be terrible if they found out this war was fixed and they had to fight it over again,

They cant let the Russians in this league or they would make a Bush League out of it,

The Peace Conference

Best time to have formed this League of Nations was during the war when all these Nations needed each other,

Everybody is for something to prevent war, but they are afraid it is like Prohibition it dont prohibit,

League of Nations just as clear as the Income Tax blanks,

One thing we got to be thankful for our Soldiers can win wars faster than our Diplomats can talk us into them,

Pres Wilson finally got discouraged at the stalling and told them that if they dident hurry up and do something the Americans would pick up their Wives and come home,

Pres says "JAMES BRING MY BOAT"[43]

They then got busy and decided that Belgium could try the Kaiser, Belgium said "how do we get him," Allies said "thats it if we could get him we would try him ourselves,"

Some Nations got so tired waiting for Peace they went back to fighting again,[44]

Been working on this League of Nations all winter, Finally one of the deligates said "What about Peace with Germany" The others all said "thats right we never thought of that,"

Went to call in Germany and they said "Why we had give you all up thought you wasent coming, We got a better offer from the Bolsheveki"[45]

They offer us no indemnities and no Baths,

If they ever have another war lets have it understood before they start what each Nation wants at the finish,

All those Nations claim they were fighting for freedom, But of course a little more land would make a little more Freedom,

One thing about this League, The last war there were only 10 to 15 nations in it now if they all sign this they can all be in the next one, It wont be near so exclusive,

Course its hard to please everybody Taft tried that,

If Pres Wilson had any doubts about this League of Nations being put through he

should have taken some of these Prohibi-
tionist. They would have shown him how
to get it through whether people wanted it
or not,

France says they would have more confidence in this League if they would slip a
couple of Nations in between them and
Germany,

I WONDER IF WE QUIT FIGHTING TOO QUICK
AND DIDENT SIGN PEACE QUICK ENOUGH,

Dont get impatient. It has been just this
hard at the end of every war to try and prevent another one,

Pres on his last voyage home said the
Monroe Doctrine was fully protected already
And to show them that it was, He has now
put it in,

The Monroe thing the Republicans talk
so much of and know so little about, Protects
us again everything but VILLA.[46]

And in the whole History of America he
is the only *Nation* that ever attacked us,

Italy says they will pick up their Marbles
and go home

23

Pres Wilson says you may Fiume, But you will never get it,[47]

Today is Japans day to threaten to pack their kimonas and leave,[48]

Italy bases her claim on an old treaty, She cant afford to trace her Treatys back too far, *If I remember she originally was signed up with Germany,*

Pres Wilson certainly used good judgement in visiting Italy when he first went over,

Sectry BAKER has gone back over to France again think old Newt, kinder likes PARIS,[49]

They wanted Mcadoo to go but the salary wasent right,

Can you imagine a guy that couldent make a living out of all the jobs he held, I would love to have just half what one Republican would have made out of all that,[50]

Lot of Reps dont want this League Gag to pass they are jealous cause the Democrats ran the last war, And they want to have another one to show how much better they could run one than the Democrats,

Even the Big 4 seem to be losing confidence, They have removed the words High Contracting Parties, which appeared 418 times in the original and now speak of it meekly as members of the League,

We know Pres Wilson had a lot to do with drafting it, Cause it has so many WORDS

Now it will take longer to explain it than it did to write it,

If Mr Lodge and Mr Lowell debate on these new amendments Boston has applied for a change of Venue,[51]

Only debate ever held where both men agreed,

Pres is up to his old tricks has sent a NOTE to Italy,

His appeal to the Italian People caused as much of a furore as the one to the voters last fall,

Italy says they know Fiume was not in their secret treaty with other Allies But its a nice town and they hate to see it fall into bad hands,

Get all those Nations sore enough to start telling the truth about each other, We will hear something,

Italy claims Fiume because there is more Italians there than anybody else, according to that Look whod get NEW YORK

Japans claims are sorter novel "They want pay for capturing part of China one of our own Allies"

They have offered to protect Siberia if they have to stay there forever to do it,

If Japan gets all her claims China will pay more indemnities than Germany who lost the war,

Imagine Japan, Pres Wilson, and Italy, All talking at once, Good thing they cant understand each other or this Conference would never have lasted this long,

AND THEY CALL THAT A PEACE CONFERENCE,

Guess those CZECHO POLOKS have gotten their freedom, I see where they are at *war*.

Wish I could find a man who had read this
LEAGUE OF NATIONS, And could tell which
was the *Assembly* and which was the *Council,*

Thats a good clause in there "where any
Allied Nation must give three months notice
before it jumps onto any other Allied
Nation,"

*Now the Women want to send Deligates,
They forget this is a* Peace Conference,

See where the German Deligates to the
Peace Table brought their Golf Clubs We
can see now how Admiral Graysons Pupil[52]
stacks up against opposition,

See where Pres Wilson and Italy have
compromised on that town down there *Italy
got it,*

Its kinder new wrinkle in Diplomacy, The
Slovaks can play with it four years till they
begin to like it, And then they take it away
from them,

AS I UNDERSTAND IT ITALY IS TO HAVE IT
TUESDAYS AND SATURDAYS,

But they are going to build those other
People *(with that terrible name)* A little

27

young town just as much like this one as they can, down the river aways

Guess the reason they put a four year limit on it, Was that they figured that would about cover the existence of any of those new Nations,

The Idea over there now seems to be lets get something ready to sign up, Whether its any good or not,

See where Pres Wilson and Japan *compromised* on the CHOW CHOW PLACE JAPAN GETS IT,[53]

I dont know how much money Indemnity Japan will demand from China,

You know CHINA *has one of the best* JAPANESE *Armies in the World,*

See where Pres Wilson and England compromised on Freedom of the Seas England got it,

Italy left the Conference and got what she wanted, Japan threatened to leave and got what she wanted, If Pres Wilson had left some Republican Senators would have gotten what they wanted,

Seems several Nations were like Jesse Willard *they wanted to know what they were to get before they entered the Arena,*[54]

Well they finally handed Germany the Peace terms 80 thousand words only thing ever written longer than a Lafollette Speech,[55]

HAD TO BE THAT LONG TO TELL THE GERMANS WHAT THEY THOUGHT OF THEM

Imagine what a document for Lawers to pick flaws in,

Could have settled the whole thing in one sentence, "IF YOU BIRDS START ANYTHING AGAIN WE WILL GIVE YOU THE OTHER BARREL,"

RUSSIA cant get in on this Peace There is not enough Paper in the World to print 80 thousand Russian words on,

If they want to get even with Germany they ought to let them keep their Cables And appoint Burleson to run them

I thought the Armistace terms read like a second Mortgage, But this reads like a FORECLOSURE,

If Germany ever wants to go to war again she will have to fight with *BEER STEINS*

If Germany stops to read those 80 thousand words before they sign them, We needent expect Peace to be signed for years yet,

Now Folks with all this kidding and foolishness aside, for I just say in here whatever I think anybody might laugh at, But of course my real sentiments are the same as everybody else, anything to prevent war If He puts this thing through and there is no more wars, His address will be WHITE HOUSE WASHINGTON D C till his whiskers are as long as the Peace Treaty If it should be a Fliv, (which it wont) Why then a letter would reach him at ALABI NEW JERSEY. So all Credit to Pres Wilson it took some game Guy to go through with it,

THE END

NOTES

[1]Rogers refers here and elsewhere to wartime conservation programs. Americans joined in a volunteer food rationing program which Herbert Hoover directed. Fuel, gas, paper, string, and all types of materials were saved to aid the war effort.

[2]McGuffey's Readers were a series of textbooks compiled by William Holmes McGuffey (1800-1873). These *Readers* were standard fare in the elementary schools of America during the nineteenth century. Will Rogers jokingly claimed that he never advanced beyond the fourth reader in the series.

[3]Edward Mandell House (1858-1938). Confidant of President Wilson. Influenced the Democratic nomination of Wilson in 1912 and served as Wilson's closest advisor. Member of the U.S. peace commission after World War I, and helped draft the covenant of the League of Nations. When Wilson was absent from Paris, House replaced him temporarily as the chief negotiator for the U.S.

[4](Thomas) Woodrow Wilson (1856-1924). President of the United States (1913-1921). Wilson was well-known for his political idealism; his Fourteen Points became the basis of the Paris Peace Conference. Wilson chose to represent the U.S. at the conference, thereby becoming the first President to visit Europe while in office.

[5]Friedrich Wilhelm Viktor Albert (Kaiser Wilhelm II) (1859-1941). Ruler of Germany (1888-1918). After Germany's defeat in World War I, he was exiled and lived the remainder of his life in retirement in the village of Doorn, Holland.

[6]The United Press news service reported that the armistice had been signed November 7, 1918, four days prior to the actual signing. There was a wild celebration on that day even though government officials did their best to explain that the report was premature.

[7]Union League Clubs were patriotic groups established during the Civil War throughout the North. The clubs participated in Republican politics and survived after the war in New York, Philadelphia, and Chicago as conservative social organizations. The New York Union League supported Charles Evans Hughes for president in 1916.

[8]Charles Evans Hughes (1862-1948). Governor of New York (1907-1910); associate justice of supreme court (1910-1916); secretary of state (1921-1925); chief justice of Supreme Court (1930-1941). Wilson had won a narrow victory over Hughes in the election of 1916, and papers speculated that Hughes might be chosen by the President to accompany the peace commission as the Republican representative. Ultimately, Henry White was selected as the single Republican member of the peace commission. The absence of adequate Republican representation caused considerable bitterness and was one of the tragic flaws in Wilson's design for peace.

[9]Wilhelm II had six sons and one daughter by Augusta Victoria of Schleswig-Holstein. The sons were William, Eitel, Adalbert, Augustus, Oscar, and Joachim.

[10]There was considerable speculation about who would represent the United States at the Paris Peace Conference. President Wilson waited until November 29, 1918 to make the announcement of peace commissioners. He named Secretary of State, Robert Lansing, Edward M. House, General Tasker Bliss, and Henry White. Wilson personally headed the commission. Many were dissatisfied with the selections for no congressman and only one Republican was chosen. Also accompanying President Wilson was a large entourage of specialists.

[11]Like other comics of this period, Will Rogers devised numerous jokes about the great American inventor and industrialist, Henry Ford (1863-1947), founder of the Ford Motor Company. Rogers even made a film satirizing the catastrophic changes in American life created by the flivver. Within this diplomatic setting Rogers commented about Ford's fruitless and well-publicized jaunt to Europe on a specially chartered "peace ship" he filled with "peaceniks" of all description. Rogers' inability to remember Ford's name was obviously intentional.

[12]Thomas Riley Marshall (1854-1925). Governor of Indiana (1909-1913); vice president (1913-1921). He was the first vice president to succeed himself in nearly a century and was extremely popular with the American public. He acted as ceremonial head of the U.S. while Wilson was in Paris.

[13]On January 8, 1918, President Wilson addressed Congress and suggested a program of Fourteen Points for a permanent peace. The fourteenth, and according to Wilson the most important, was the establishment of a League of Nations to promote world cooperation and hopefully to prevent another war. Wilson compromised with the Allies on all the points except the League.

[14]David Franklin Houston (1866-1940). Secretary of agriculture (1913-1920); secretary of treasury (1920-1921); President, the A & M College of Texas (1902-1905); President, University of Texas (1905-1908). He wrote *Eight Years With Wilson's Cabinet* (1926). Many thought Houston would be a member of the peace commission, but Wilson decided to substitute General Tasker Bliss.

[15]Elihu Root (1845-1937). Well-known American politician and statesman who served the United States in various political and diplomatic posts. Wilson appointed him to head a special diplomatic mission to Russia in 1917, but the president ignored the committee's report. Many advisors urged Wilson to include Root in the peace delegation as the Republican spokesman.

[16]William Jennings Bryan (1860-1925). U.S. representative from Nebraska (1891-1895); unsuccessful Democratic presidential candidate in 1896, 1900, and 1908. Leader of the party until 1912, when his influence helped nominate Woodrow Wilson. As secretary of state (1913-1915), Bryan was opposed to U.S. entry into the world conflict and when it seemed the U.S. was following a collision course, he resigned as secretary of state.

[17]Cary Travers Grayson (1878-1938). Naval officer and personal physician of President Wilson. When the President

became seriously ill at the conference, the presidential physician received considerable attention from the press. This is one of a number of cases in which Rogers relied on the newspaper reading of his audience.

[18]George Creel (1876-1953). Chairman of the Committee on Public Information (1917-1919), better known as the 'Creel Committee.' Designed to unite America in the war effort, the committee used films, posters, pamphlets, and four-minute men who made patriotic speeches to promote national unity. Creel accompanied the presidential party to Paris and was one of Wilson's personal friends.

[19]Bernard Mannes Baruch (1870-1965). American businessman and advisor to several presidents. As director of the War Industries Board (1918-1919) which controlled the economy during World War I, he was one of the most powerful men in the country. Although Baruch was considered for the position of chief negotiator during Wilson's temporary return to Washington, (February 28, 1919-March 6, 1919) Colonel House ultimately was selected.

[20]Harry Augustus Garfield (1863-1942). Fuel Administrator (1917-1919) and virtual dictator of the country's fuel resources. Increased coal production, decreed heatless days and gasless Sundays, and curtailed the use of fuel for non-war industries.

[21]Nikolai Aleksandrovich (Nicholas II) (1868-1918). Czar of Russia (1894-1917). Deposed during the Russian Revolution of 1917.

George Frederick Ernst Albert (George V) (1865-1936). King of England during World War I.

[22]Enrico Caruso (1873-1921). Italian tenor who achieved great popularity in the United States just prior to World War I. During the war Caruso sang for the Red Cross and was credited with raising $21,000,000 for the Allied Armies.

[23]Giuseppe Garibaldi (1807-1882). Italian patriot who aided in the unification of Italy. Italian reaction to any reference to Garibaldi is a good indication of the nationalistic zeal they were feeling at the conclusion of the war. This great surge of nationalism affected peace negotiations between Italy and Yugoslavia over the control of Fiume.

[24]Victor Emmanuel III (1869-1947). King of Italy (1900-1946). With the rise of Fascism, his authority declined.

[25]In October 1918 Prince Maximilian of Baden, a moderate who had replaced the former German Imperial Chancellor, wrote Wilson saying the German government requested peace based on Wilson's Fourteen Points. Wilson's answer consisted mostly of questions designed to show the German government that the peace would be concluded only on his terms. This reply to the German note was spoken of as "The President's Questionaire" by Rogers.

[26]William Ashley "Billy" Sunday (1862-1935). Evangelist who reached the peak of his career between 1910-1920. He strongly supported the passage of the eighteenth amendment providing for national prohibition.

[27]Rogers probably referred to the fact that Mexico did not participate actively in the war and the German Crown

35

Prince, although a military officer, was not reputed to be a good wartime leader.

[28]In February Wilson made a visit to the United States to sign bills of the expiring 65th Congress and to explain in person the draft of the League Covenant to the members of the Senate and House Committees on Foreign Affairs. He returned to France in March to resume discussions.

[29]Woodrow Wilson's quotation of this line on two occasions and the effects of this presidential attention are described in the introduction to this volume.

[30]Wilson arrived at the Paris Peace Conference with a comprehensive blueprint for peace. He was completely unaware that the allies were prevented from honoring his Fourteen Points because of secret treaties they had signed during some of the darker days of the war. Wilson's idealistic Fourteen Points could make little progress against entrenched interests and the European desire to punish Germany.

[31]James Hamilton Lewis (1863-1939). U. S. representative from Washington (1897-1898); U. S. senator from Illinois (1913-1919, 1931-1939). Best known for his extravagant dress. Besides this sartorial peculiarity he was known as an excellent parliamentary tactician and twice served as majority whip.

[32]Albert Sidney Burleson (1863-1937). U. S. representative from Texas (1899-1913); postmaster general (1913-1921). As postmaster general during the war he banned mail critical of the government. He served as chairman of the U.S. Telegraph and Telephone Administration, and later supported public ownership of these industries.

[33]Rogers referred to Henry Cabot Lodge's leadership of Senate opposition to the League of Nations. Lodge and others signed a document proclaiming that they would not support the proposed League of Nations if the League were included as part of the peace treaty. Although Rogers used the term "Wilful 37", thirty-nine senators signed the resolution.

[34]William Gibbs McAdoo (1863-1941). U.S. secretary of the treasury (1913-1919); director-general of railroads (1917-1919) when they were being run by the government; unsuccessfully sought Democratic nomination for president (1920, 1924); U.S. senator from California (1933-1939). Married Eleanor Wilson, daughter of President Wilson (1914).

[35]William Howard Taft (1857-1930). President of the United States (1909-1913); chief justice of the Supreme Court (1921-1930); secretary of war (1904-1908). On March 4, 1919, Taft and Wilson spoke at the New York Metropolitan Opera House in support of the League of Nations.

[36]Josephus Daniels (1862-1948). Editor of the *Raleigh* (North Carolina) *State Chronicle* (1885-1894) and *News and Observer* (1894-1933). Secretary of the Navy (1913-1921); U. S. ambassador to Mexico (1933-1941). Authored *The Wilson Era* (1944).

[37]Herbert Clark Hoover (1874-1964). U.S. food administrator (1917-1919); Chairman of Commission for

Relief in Belgium (1915-1919); in charge of relief in eastern European countries (1921); secretary of commerce (1921-1928); president of U. S. (1929-1933). As food administrator Hoover instituted wheatless Mondays and Wednesdays, meatless Tuesdays, and porkless Thursdays and Saturdays. The volunteer belt-tightening program was called "hooverizing."

[38]Rogers referred to Wisconsin's large German population and the growing anti-German feelings in the United States. During the war the manufacture of liquor was carefully regulated and even intermittently forbidden. Many German-Americans protested this action, for they believed that the manufacture of liquors was neither unnecessary nor unpatriotic.

[39]In 1914 the British gave Ireland home rule, but the outbreak of World War I prevented it from taking effect. Irish rebels wanting complete independence from England and expecting German aid, led a revolt on Easter Sunday, 1916. The German ship carrying arms to Ireland was intercepted, leaders were arrested, and the rebellion collapsed. The Armistice of 1918 did not bring peace in Ireland, for in 1919 when Ireland declared independence war erupted with England.

[40]After it proved impossible for the large number of delegates meeting in Paris to work effectively, a Council of Ten was delegated to draft the terms of peace. However, the critical decisions were made by the Big Four, Woodrow Wilson, David Lloyd George, Georges Clemenceau, and Vittorio Orlando.

David Lloyd George (1863-1945). Prime minister of Great Britain, lawyer, orator, and world traveler who headed the British delegation to Paris. Lloyd George had been returned to power in 1918 on the strength of his party's firm attitude toward Germany.

Georges Eugene Benjamin Clemenceau (1841-1929). Prime minister of France (1906-1909, 1917). Was chairman of the Paris Peace Conference. Called the 'Tiger of France' and had won a vote of confidence in the Chamber of Deputies by a resolve to prevent future German threats to French security.

Vittorio Emanuele Orlando (1860-1952). Prime minister (1917-1919), headed the Italian delegation to the Paris Peace Conference. Orlando was concerned mainly with territorial concessions and when he was not able to achieve the territory he claimed for Italy, his ministry was overthrown.

[41]In February, 1917, Japan, England, and the other major Allied powers (excepting the United States) signed a treaty giving German islands north of the equator to Japan, and islands south of the line to England. Japan also would acquire German rights in China. Serious disagreement ensued when Japan also demanded Kiaochow in the Shantung province of China.

[42]Monroe Doctrine. The doctrine stated that the United States would not allow foreign colonization of the Western Hemisphere. Many opponents of the League of Nations

argued that the League's covenant would destroy the exclusive American right to enforce the Monroe Doctrine in the Western Hemisphere.

[43]President Wilson sailed from New York for Paris December 4, 1918 on board the *George Washington*. In April, 1919, Wilson ordered the *George Washington* back to France and considered ending American participation, for the Allies refused to follow his program.

[44]At the end of the war, many smaller nations engaged in territorial disputes while the negotiators were attempting to redraw the map of Europe along nationalistic lines. Greece and Turkey were quarreling and the newly created country of Czechoslavakia was received with hostility by Hungary and Poland.

[45]In 1917, the Russians signed the Treaty of Brest-Litovsk ending war with Germany. The treaty was humiliating to the Russians for they were forced to surrender territory including Finland, the Baltic States, Poland, and the Ukraine.

[46]Francisco (Pancho) Villa (1877-1923). Mexican revolutionary figure who crossed the American border to attack Columbus, New Mexico. When he learned that some Americans had been killed, President Wilson sent troops under John J. Pershing into Mexican territory to pursue the Mexican raider. The American counterattack was sharply criticized and proved unsuccessful. Villa was later assassinated by his own people.

[47]Italy wanted the port of Fiume but other powers at Paris thought the area should go to Yugoslavia. Wilson would not support the Italian claims; he sought Italian public opinion for his program. All he succeeded in doing was angering the Italian delegation. The controversy raged throughout the conference and a workable compromise was not reached. The failure of Orlando to gain this area for Italy prompted his overthrow. Later in 1919, Fiume was captured by an Italian poet D'Annunzio and a patroit army. This seizure was confirmed by a treaty between Mussolini and the Yugoslav government in 1924.

[48]The Japanese wanted recognition of their claims to former German territory in the Shantung Province of China; if they did not win agreement they implied that they would follow the Italians and withdraw from the conference.

[49]Newton D. Baker (1871-1937). Mayor of Cleveland, Ohio (1912-1916); U. S. secretary of war (1916-1921); member, Permanent Court of Arbitration at the Hague. As secretary of war Baker proved his ability by drafting, training, and transporting American troops overseas in a short time. When the peace commission was first chosen, Baker was to replace Wilson when the President returned to the United States, but Colonel House was chosen instead. Baker's visit to the troops in France in 1919 was one of the most discussed events of his career.

[50]In January, 1919, Secretary of Treasury McAdoo's health and personal finances, strained by his years in government service, prompted his resignation. During the war he also had been chairman of the Federal Reserve Board, the Federal Farm Loan Board, and the War Finance Corporation, and Director General of Railroads.

[51]On March 19, 1919 Senator Henry Cabot Lodge (1850-1924) of Massachusetts and President A. Lawrence Lowell of Harvard University (1856-1943) debated on the wisdom of the proposed League of Nations. Lodge represented the negative and Lowell the affirmative, although Lowell also believed some revisions should be incorporated. Governor Calvin Coolidge presided over the Boston debate.

[52]To maintain the President's health, Admiral Grayson, the presidential physician prescribed the popular new sport of golf.

[53]There was considerable debate at the Conference over who should control the Kiaochow area. In the end, the treaty granted Japan the unexpired German lease of Kiaochow. Wilson agreed to the Japanese demands only after they promised their stay in China would be temporary.

[54]Jess Willard (1881-1968). Former heavyweight boxing champion who won the title from Jack Johnson and lost it to Jack Dempsey, both controversial fights. Willard fought Johnson in Havana; although Willard won the match Johnson later stated he had thrown the fight. Dempsey won the title from Willard in 1919. Willard was an ex-Oklahoma cowpuncher and eventually performed with 101 Ranch Wild West Show.

[55]Robert M. LaFollette (1855-1925). U. S. representative from Wisconsin (1885-1891); governor of Wisconsin (1901-1906); U. S. senator (1906-1925). Ran for president in 1924 on the Progressive party ticket. Died in 1925 and was replaced in the Senate by his son, Robert M. LaFollette, Jr.

FROM HEMP TO VERBAL LARIAT

Americans in the first two decades of the twentieth century were fascinated by the image of the cowboy, for he symbolized the nation's last frontier experience before America became an industrialized nation. Will Rogers capitalized on this interest in things western as a participant in Wild West shows and as a vaudeville performer (1902 to 1926). In the earliest phase of his career, Rogers' act emphasized his manual dexterity with the lasso. If comedy was ever a part of his western act, the comedy was based on physical movement rather than verbal wit.

Rogers transformed his act into something more than a display of roping before he joined Florenz Ziegfeld's Follies in 1915. Rogers realized that to survive his act would have to rise to the urbanity of his late-night audience. The rope remained in

throwing two ropes at once.

In the earliest phase of his career, Rogers'
act emphasized his dexterity with a lasso.

the act, but emphasis began to move in favor of
commentary about news items in the day's press.
And if these items involved distinguished patrons
of the *Follies,* all the better! Rogers' audience was
delighted by the way in which this deceptively
simple and naive plainsman could ensnare the most
perplexing issues with his verbal lariat. The rope
was no longer a utilitarian tool, but a metaphor for
Rogers' ability to satirize the foibles and pretensions
of men in power.

Will Rogers was elevated to a national plane as

His act
became
something
more than
a display
of roping
when he joined
Ziegfeld's
Follies
in 1915.

a verbal comic after a humorous confrontation with
Woodrow Wilson which is described in the introduction to this volume. Rogers was fully aware of
the portentousness of the moment: "a Warden
knocked at my dressing room door and said 'You
die in 5 minutes for kidding your country.' " The

outcome of the confrontation was far more positive than Rogers could have hoped. From that time forward, Rogers became an unofficial, humorous confidant of the succeeding American presidents (Harding, Coolidge, Hoover, Roosevelt). The tone of this privileged relationship is best summarized in an advertisement for a series of short silent films Rogers made during a European tour. The public function of his humorous advice to men in office is summarized by the caption, "Now Mr. President— This is confidential—For you—And the rest of America."

"Now, Mr. President— This is confidential— For you—And the rest of America."

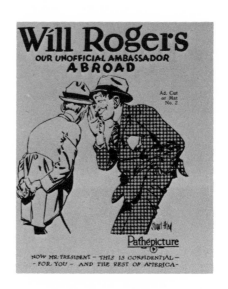

Will Rogers' advice to presidents, congressmen, and other public persons occasionally aroused strong feelings. Nevertheless, Rogers was wise enough to know that really important men were self-confident enough to enjoy his comments as long as they were conducted in the proper spirit. In introducing *The Cowboy Philosopher on the Peace Conference,* Rogers explains "That you can always

43

joke about a big man that is really big, But dont ever kid a little fellow that thinks he is something, cause he will get sore. That's why he's little." To a certain extent, Rogers was forced to adopt this style. Too many of his patrons returned to the "Midnight Frolics" night after night. Rogers was thus compelled to change his routine continuously. The device selected (at the suggestion of his wife, Betty) was to use a topical approach to events in the press.

While prominent men who were the subjects of his jokes enjoyed the humor, many observers

Prominent men
who were "lassoed"
enjoyed the humor.

Will Rogers Yanks Gov. Allen Upon Stage and Is Called 'Impertinent'

Gov. Henry Allen of Kansas was yanked out of the wings and upon the stage of the "Ziegfeld Follies" last night by Will Rogers, and the audience insisted upon a speech. Gov. Allen said that he was only one of thousands who have been delighted by Will Rogers's "impertinence," and then the Governor expressed a hope that the cowboy comedian would live forever.

"Us Oklahoma fellers never thought much of Kansas," replied Rogers. "Why, before Henry Allen took hold of the darned place it was the greatest joke State in the Union. But the Governor is a great man. Lots of Governors let their States slip back, but darned if Henry Allen did. Go on out to Kansas and see for yourself. She ain't gone back an inch. She's just the same to-day as she was when the Governor took hold of her.

"The Governor says it's good to sit down there and listen to me tell the plain truth about things. Well that ain't hard for me, being that I ain't in politics."

cringed for fear that Rogers' "impertinence" would exceed the limits of propriety. Rogers carried this style into his journalism.

As *Cowboy Philosopher on the Peace Conference* reveals, Henry Ford was often a target for Rogers humor. In fact, Rogers had more than a reading

**Will Rogers
and
Henry Ford**

acquaintance with the great inventor and industrialist. It is important to remember that Rogers' remarks about Ford were not entirely one-sided. Rogers could fantasize how these two strong-minded individualists with roots in a pre-industrial America could tune up twentieth century American life and get it back on the road.

The obvious pleasure on the faces of John D. Rockefeller and Eleanor Roosevelt is proof positive

Will Rogers with Eleanor Roosevelt *(left)* **and John D. Rockefeller** *(below).*

46

that Rogers technique warmed without burning. Will Rogers' hobnobbing with celebrities provided a service for the American mass audience. In a world of increasing social stratification and centralization of power, Rogers bridged an ever-widening psychological gap between the average American and those who shaped the laws, opinions, and fashions which affected their lives. Their gum chewing representative served to keep the national self-image coherent and humanly comprehensible. Rogers' service was especially welcomed during the stolid administrations of Harding, Coolidge, and Hoover when the presidents often seemed aloof and unconcerned with the problems of the little man.